BOTH POEMS

T0288385

BOTH POEMS

Anne Tardos

ROOF BOOKS

NEW YORK

ISBN: 978-1-931824-43-9
Library of Congress Catalog Card Number: 2011933102

Cover art by Anne Tardos, "Large Red and Yellow Ez," 1989, acrylic on linen, 34 x 48 inches (122 x 92 cm).

Author photo by Ben Sherry

Acknowledgements
Poems from this collection have appeared in *New American Writing, Poets.org (as poemflow), Web Conjunctions, Boog City, Peep / Show, Viz Journal of the Arts, Jivin' Ladybug*, and *Jacket2*.

 This book was made possible, in part, with public funds from the New York State Council on the Arts, a state agency.
NYSCA

Roof Books are distributed by
Small Press Distribution
1341 Seventh Street
Berkeley, CA. 94710-1403
Phone orders: 800-869-7553
www.spdbooks.org

Roof Books are published by
Segue Foundation
300 Bowery
New York, NY 10012
seguefoundation.com

for Michael Byron

CONTENTS

PRONOUNCE

2009

All

Love is found in all the ways friends speak.

The thing is that we all just fall apart.

Just look at all that stuff!

All events that occur are caused by earlier events. An idea for a
form originates from another form. You could say, being alive means
defending a form.

All the walks I've taken in New York. I owe it all.

Another

Now is a strong time in my life. Another time would have been another story.

Another option would have been not to be born at all, not to be trapped on this carousel, laughing incomprehensibly, as it hurtles along its circularity.

But then I wouldn't have been around to be thinking this.

I straighten my back a little.

There.

Anything

I'm going to the store, do you need anything?

Anything-in-itself.

Anything does not go. It stays and weighs its options. It leaves no traces because it barely exists as a thing, only as a thinly floating hint of a concept of a possibility or a subsidiary potential, resisting attempts at definition.

Anything does not go.

Anything whatsoever and everything else, including a slumbering kangaroo who is into wordless thinking.

I'd give anything to be with you.

Both

Both of them enjoyed a progressively changing quality to their consciousness. Efforts to avoid one another and their egoistic desires affected them both.

They both agreed on severing all ligaments: one cut ties out of carelessness and confusion, the other, as a response. Both washed their hands of one another.

They both regarded their actions as primary and their states of mind as less important. While they both suffered as well as benefited from each other's actions, their states of mind often remained secret and felt to be inaccessible.

They both knew how to keep silent.
They both knew how to show off.
I think they both missed the point.

Each other

Like two maladjusted magnets, they were at each other's throats.

Their universe, filled with the total activity of life, appeared to them in each moment, and there was no standing still.

They held each other's hands, gently tightening their grip in an effort to keep each other from crying.

They were headed to a cabin by a lake in a pine forest where they found each other's happiness.

Everyone / Everybody

Everyone is potentially everyone else: inseparable and
distinguished.

Everyone makes assertions, names numbers, and declares
mathematical objects to exist independently of the human mind, and
everyone aligns all discourse along multiple staves of the score.

Common sense is direct and primitive. Everyone knows this.

Everyone apportions their belief to the evidence they have, but
some have difficulties formalizing the evidential support. Everyone
relies on many unformalizable assumptions.

And then everybody gets stoned.

Everything

Everything you seek is guided by what is sought.

Everything frightens me. Every little sound out of the ordinary that might signal something off kilter in some way, worries me, affects my already shaky state of mind in some terrifying way. Everything is a threat to my throat and a menace to my mental state.

Then again, everything could be said to be full of beauty and a potential source of happiness. Everything could be seen as a privilege, a fantastic adventure.

Everything needs to be categorized and distinguished, subdivided into *kinds* and *modes*, into particulars and universals, having concrete and abstract properties.

When you find yourself in ill thoughts, stop everything but breathing.

Everything is empty.

Few

Few understand how hopelessly trapped they are inside those little bodies of theirs. And only a few have kindness in them.

Being tightly enclosed and isolated entities, few will ever venture outside their own skin.

Few accept the fact that decline is not only a side effect of their being, but the very essence of their journey. And although the process is being referred to as "decline," the motion is in fact a forward one, an exponential progression along the path initially taken.

More than a few manage to find solace in an order they know is illusory.

Few will see reality in such brutally realistic ways that even fewer among them will manage to survive their devastating insight.

The few, who don't keep their built-in, invisible, yet palpable distance, transgressing and blundering into others' territories, are probably not well versed in the art of restraint.

He

Abruptness is the exigency of a decorative man who fears embarrassment.

Solitary and terrible, he skips tenderness.

Hatred and compassion act as the connective tissue of his poetic vocabulary.

He classifies in order to refer. He refers in order to reach. The act of reaching propels him in that the reached-for object approaches him with equal velocity, and as he pulls it toward himself, it, too, pulls him toward itself, past and across everything else he didn't reach for.

He navigates within an order he created, which is part of an order he did not create.

Seeking dignity, he sees his battle as lost and his grave as dug.

He draws a fine line between a fine line and a fine line.

Him

I love him. Like the woman who, in her search for masculine strength, falls for ruthless cads, unyielding dads, I love him.

My parents, who barely survived the Nazi persecution for being Jews, communists, and members of the French Resistance, sometimes would look at me with great concern, and say "*fais gaffe à toi!*"which is French slang for "Be careful out there!"

Then they each went their own way and left me standing there.

I do what I can.

All I've experienced up to now is forming the next moment of comprehension.

His

So she knocks on his door and, as he motions her in, she explains that she came over primarily to suck him off—if he would let her—although she would prefer that he didn't come into her mouth. You know, would you be able to withdraw just in time? Why not? He would shrug, and rolling his eyes, he might turn away in disgust, thinking, oh, why must I deal with such people? And he would unbuckle his belt with that certain loathing he had learned to not only live with, but even take comfort in, in the course of his difficult life.

Loosening the strictures around the linguistic organization of symbolic renewal and joy, and calling into question the psyche and the world, she discovers that the very size of his penis is exactly right for her mouth.

Fear of becoming subject to unwieldy sentiments is being met by monomaniacal rites of purification. No, darling, he would murmur, not just yet, not now.

What do I mean when I say "I love you"?

The infant sucks the mother's breast
The adult, the father's penis

Not to mention all the details and variations.

I

I train my mind to concentrate.
I look for one-pointed thought.
I avoid selfishness and vanity.

I work out my salvation with diligence.

I begin and I persevere.

I'm not afraid of casting pearls before swine.

I kill out desire. I walk on. I deny nothing. I affirm all.

I become who I am.

It

It means everything to me. I owe it so much. Then again, whatever it is, I'm against it.

It's impossible. It varies.

It listens. It's a force to be reckoned with.

You adapt to it. It adapts to you.

It's at your service. It can happen. It happens.

In fact, it never fails.

It will take its toll.
Fuck it.

What it means to be: It means a forward and outward, ever expanding motion that leads to a gradual and seemingly total dissolution before eventually being reformed, or reconstituted, as we would call it.

It really doesn't care what you call it.

One thing is certain: use it *and* lose it.

Many

Many gain strength from something inside themselves. They discover things about their real selves and don't allow anxiety to veil their world.

Many see themselves as points in an uncontrollable life-pattern of immeasurable dimensions.

Familiar routines and rote responses thrust many into a rut.

And many are wondering what went wrong with the supercollider.

Me

Know me as a mode of substance rather than a bundle of perceptions.

See me in terms of contradictions and know me as I couldn't know myself.

The Me that will wake tomorrow cannot be the same as the Me that falls asleep tonight.

My personal identity is tied to its substance: my body, my brain, and their connectedness.

Understand me as a continuity rather than a changelessness.

Call me.

My

My role as a form is to seek other forms, merge with them, as events unfold.

My enthusiasm, doubt, and pleasure of inquiry into the meaning of language or the architecture of an idea help me understand that some lessons are unlearnable.

My studied languors, my voluptuous distress, my ecstatic sufferings, my twitchings, my nervous tremours, my spasms, my screams, my grimaces, my sugared, sickly smiles and kisses, my sneaking gestures and insinuating remarks, my hoarse, lewd whisperings.

Myself

So deep is the imagery that I may not always know if I'm regarding myself as myself or as an image.

I see myself as divided, like a musical composition that draws attention to my desire for satisfaction by refusing to give it.

I paint my identity in a light that elevates me above the mean cravings I'm subject to.

Everyone I've ever been, I am now.

Neither

Neither one of us knew how things would turn out. Neither one of us could have existed without the other.

We study each other and forget ourselves. We become attached to the transient expression of our true nature.

Imbalance and disorder define neither the straight nor the narrow.

Neither makes me think of Either/Or, which makes me think of Both, which makes me think of All.

And All is where I began.

Nobody

Nobody wants to hear that death can always come in the next minute yet everyone accepts the premise.

Nobody never nothing is more important than anybody ever anything.

Nobody thinks of a tiny crevice as a moment in time.

Nobody knows anything.

Nobody is waiting for me.

Nobody ever loved anyone the way everyone wants to be loved.

Nothing

Nothing exists in isolation. We arise and perish within a network of relationships with everything else.

The nothingness that is the negation of being, must itself be negated.

I deny nothing.

Nothing as incoherent as the notion of a spiritual authority.

Nothing.

Other

Twitter ripped the veil off the Other—and we saw ourselves.

We need the Other to confirm that we exist.

If the other desists, I demur.

Others may hold other opinions.

Our

Our conscience communicates the meaning of nothingness by keeping silent.

Desire itself becomes more important than its object.

Self-indulgent feelings of guilt become substitutes for action, and compromise our experience.

The question is how do we reset things to zero. Because every time zero comes up, we can take another breath. So I guess every time we exhale up to the point we inhale, there is a moment of zero when no air seems to go in or out. It's a finite moment, contained within our infinity.

I say our infinity, as I would say our solar system or our galaxy.

Ourselves

We fear ourselves, because if we can kill and destroy, ingest and assimilate another entity, who knows, we could be next.

We find ourselves increasingly in control as we progress, until we reach a new and unfamiliar terrain, where we could easily fall down if we didn't use our imagination.

By conceptualizing various possibilities, imagination aids us in negotiating a potentially chaotic situation. Another path it can take us is straight down the abyss.

Several

Several is one of those words that is difficult for me to pronounce,
no doubt due to my non-anglophonic origins.

Larry Rivers gave me a lot of trouble with his ri-ri.
Larry I can do. Rivers is no problem. But Larry Rivers is hard for me.

My first "r" was the French *rigolo, ravissant, escargot, ratatouille.*
Then I learned the Hungarian one with its *répa retek mogyoró korán
reggel ritkán rikkant a rigó.* And then the German *Sprache, Marx,
Strudelhofstiege.* And finally the radiant articulation of the English "r,"
that semivowel, that glide.

She

Her reason for being was that she existed. A death seemed like a small price to pay.

She predicted her future by referring to past experiences. The flaws of this method were repeatedly demonstrated to her by past experiences of false predictions. If she wanted some sort of realism, she had to undermine her predictive notions with doubt, take her own conclusions with a grain of salt, and expertly slip in and out of her social, ideological, and intellectual constructs.

It's not like she had too many options.

Crawling on hands and knees through mud and filth and sexual perverts, drugs and smoke and toxic drinks, the humiliation of poverty and physical pain, she finally reached a place of clarity and humanity, where she could collect herself before continuing her journey.

She was well on her way.

Some

Feeling themselves to be different from others, some believe one moment to be more significant than another.

Free of interpretation and subject-object, mind-body complication, some associations go beyond the reach of reason.

Some of the hardness of egotism is overcome by dissolving illusions.

It's alright for some.

Something

Something is somehow a questioning of something.

Sleep being slept, a bird has something to say.

A burden of solitude.

A simulacrum, a mirror, a puppet, a tool by which I gauge my imagination, exercise my emotions, as if they were muscles in need of flexing.

Something makes me endure who you are.

Their

Ever notice how their eyes look up as soon as they put food into their mouths?

As soon as the nourishment enters the oral cavity, before their teeth could come down on it, their eyes will shoot up straight ahead, fiercely protecting their prey. Their jaws and teeth are dominant, and they only let go of things once they deem their time as having come.

In reality, however, their time is always there.
They are, in fact, their own time at all times.

Life and death are not separable, but occur simultaneously within each moment, instantaneously and unthinkingly. Together they constitute their own total dynamic.

Each instant covers the entire world.

Knowing this, they cling to and affirm their lives, and they fear and negate their deaths.

As they should.

Themselves

To free themselves of themselves, they overcome the hardness of their egotism by dissolving their illusions.   Simple.

They are disposed to think favorably of themselves. This helps them withstand the rigors of life.

The walls of the Museum of the Self are covered with mirrors and self-reflective portraits.

Exercising continuous control over themselves, they ask themselves: "do I really love this person?"

They

They lie to me. They think I need to be lied to. Their disingenuousness comes naturally to them. They are shifty and clever. They outsmart me almost every time.

They take advantage of me. They refuse to take me into their hearts. They forget that I am here to ease their journey. They forget that I am one of them.

Even death can't soothe their aching hearts.

Us

Who counts as one of us? All of us, who are motivated by pleasure and pain. Humans, parrots, sharks, Alpha Centaurians.

Give us our daily bread and shut up.

Life doesn't just happen to us, we happen to it.

Our personal identity is arbitrary in that we become who we are, instead of becoming somebody else.

Everyone is potentially everyone else: inseparable and distinguished.

What we make of all this stuff is up to us.

I mean, look at us.

We Are Building This Thing Together

We know better than to fall head over heels. We are being cautious, apprehensive, and fearful. We abdicate, resign, step down. We escape. We avoid. We lose willingly. The art of losing is our expertise.

Our bitterness is dark. Sticky, viscous, and established. The kind you scrape off a vanilla bean or the black goo inside a pipe.

Ominous and tempting, our fingertips tingle
Our noses unkissed
And our suffering, we're told, is self willed.

What

What is being asked about contains that which is to be found out by the asking.

If I see the real world as a colorless and largely qualityless source from which the world I experience emanates, I do so from the viewpoint of a world full of color and quality.

What I see and hear represents what *is* as well as what I *think* is.

Descartes says we don't know that we are fully dressed because we cannot distinguish the state of being dressed from that of being naked while dreaming that we are dressed.

Perceptual error makes us unable to distinguish hallucination from genuine perception.

In other words, what is fabricated and what isn't.

Who

Who likes being thrown overboard suddenly and without warning?

Who enjoys being carelessly tossed aside?

And who, for that matter, would want to be the one committing these offenses?

I mean who needs this shit?

I don't know who you are.

You

You fear me.

You trust no one.

You fear the very air you breathe.

You're   so   vain.

Stimuli affecting you from the very beginning of your life, and before, come from others. You are others. When you die, others die.

You use language as a prisoner uses confinement and a builder uses walls, living within and without.

Little by little, you prepare your thoughts.

Fresh and innocent you are.

     You call me by my name.

     I love You.

NINE 1–63

2009–2011

Nine words per line and nine lines per stanza.

Pink fluffy underwater kangaroo fuzzy free manic rabbity thing.

Sense and nonsense similarly writer's block clogged and unblocked.

Happiness nothing really blue so you can start living.

Laptop immersion fools your brain into thinking whatever needed.

Gazebo-tranquility-ragweed, condemned to live with the self.

Find yourself totally isolated strict exile a common ploy.

Like you, I'm impatient as we become each other.

Bright green primary features evolving society—the age thing.

Sleep being slept, a bird has something to say.

Reality flip flop artistic failure extremely hard to explain.

Foggy zendo vigilance gendergap understanding the desire to live.

Levitating underbelly slime, dengue fever ankle deep, vilification zigzag.

I love you too dear—count your chickens carefully.

Echochamber plantlife indoor cellular reality busy yellow rent abatement.

Quiet knucklehead comradery a thousand hopes subject to change.

Infinity appears in repeated mirror images perceived as reflection.

Zealous devotion to waxwork sex, because Sigmund said so.

Birthing velocity's snapshot-like nature, pushed to the extreme.

It is Racine not Montaigne for many lovers' discourse.

To suddenly fall upon the old dialectic of enlightenment.

And what is masturbation if not a homosexual act?

A role to play must have a visible function.

We are being categorized in the realm of tonality.

A counterintuitive yearning for the quiescence of pre-birth.

The way our twig's bent is how we grow.

Empty thermos, unkissed nosetip, text rotation, and marsupial nesting.

Kerchief ligament pirouette darkness jettison mother of
  invention boy-toy.

Zany foxy smoke alarm tremolo evacuation juniper ginger dimple.

Zinguer je je zinguer je, mich dich Villa nicht.

Every thought first thought in the visible universe, strange.

Zendo cushion run for it go. Long ago Labrador.

Swift recollection tired Daphne just like our overheated relationshit.

Something has changed I felt giddy I felt sick.

Since women. Forget it. No way. Barbaric and inhumane.

Learning a lot here: I'm wrong in being wrong.

Djibouti laptop polyrhythmic stevedore imagination for example
  people die.

Yeah yeah yeah listen to the music around you.

Plagiarize and cannibalize yourself by mining your own work.

Counter-sadistic anti-suffering *vraiment triste faché* becoming real.

Don't think for a minute that you don't exist.

First, get used to the sound of my voice.

Bob Perelman knows what Maisie knew about her parents.

Katy Lederer didn't have money. She was a poet.

Mitch Highfill keeps a pet moth and an elephant.

Dirty birthday, suntan-benevolence of impenetrable and
incendiary nature.

Vibrations and particularized energy formations make some
sense somehow.

Mind-independent reality: Haley's Comet exists even if we don't.

Hold your lover's hand, and tomorrow will be yesterday.

When in ill thoughts again, stop everything but breathing.

Life is cool. Nothing need be done about it.

Jewish reconstructionism in Mamaroneck, why just a
minute ago.

When out of context, nothing will ever make sense.

Now I understand you because now I love you.

Mix of funk and freejazz Miles Davis musical response.

Lucretius saw the universe as something having a nature.

Bernstein: "Estrangement is our home ground," Yukon bullfrog flu.

Barely arrived, it seems, and almost time to leave.

If narrowness were the price of intensity—not necessarily.

Adeena Karasick textacy and her rules of textual engagement.

Segue Zen coffee house Segue haunted lightning Segue offerings.

Place holders and temporary solutions require tolerance trust imagination.

Rachel Zolf Israeli-Palestinian Lesbian writing methods her Gematria.

Filling what is empty—it does keep getting better.

Dubious fanatical relationship-focus brilliant thinking interesting,
  I write.

Cleverly observed in retrospect via dark tunnels to New Jersey.

Honesty because it's easier and honesty because it's easier.

All of a sudden we can't be far behind.

Together we can be keen, intelligent, well-meaning, and visible.

Like two shadows, never to be overtaken by anyone.

I quietly become agitated like a storm-tossed ship.

Now I'll confess something to you: I don't know.

How utterly abominable. How can you be so callous?

That cute smile and that glimmer in your eyes.

Bill Luoma uses the word "raw" as a noun.

Just look at all that raw covering his neurasthenia.

How his neurons respond to stimuli with exaggerated force.

"Let me listen to *me*, and not to them."

Thinking of you brings me to my knees with longing.

Life could be seen as some kind of spasm.

Smitten in mid-spill the baby and the bathwater.

10

First you practice nonviolence on *yourself* then on others.

All events that occur are caused by earlier events.

An idea for a form originates from another form.

You could say, "being alive means defending a form."

These phone calls are strong enthusiastic and uniquely restrictive.

Anguish chagrin discomfort despair grief depression guilt and
remorse.

A group of gentle friends and their mixed emotions.

Is Nothing the inertia of Something, asks a friend.

I'm confessing that I love you, now, this minute.

We try subdividing space and time into infinite segments.

Our apparently random behavior fits within a deterministic system.

We run around like titillated and tantalized windup toys.

"We feel and we know that we are eternal."

If we understood infinity, suicide would have to fail.

We know nothing as uncertain as a sure thing.

Feeling happy can be as gentle as sipping water.

Even a hedonist must have *some* concern for others.

How they managed to dirty the very word "liberal."

Marxist writing, Marxist writing, woman's work is never done.

My view of reality is vague if I'm vague.

Why can't scientific research ever reach a perfect truth?

The purest moment of perversion and its clandestine sites.

Tranquil moment in the life of a northern town.

I look at the page and I start writing.

Dog drives car—breaks the rules—wrinkle, Volvo, sniff.

I loved you in the middle of the afternoon.

Carey's 6-word poem: "Oh Mom, it is so beautiful."

"There's no way to peace—peace is the way."

Miles Davis says play what you *don't* know.

Everything we seek is guided by what is sought.

Sources of my knowledge are sensation, memory, introspection,
reason.

Every thought is first thought, and also best thought.

I feel obligated to live as excellently as possible.

A phony Somali passport and a screechy mythological gargoyle.

This elasticity is overrated, so don't mention it again.

Dripping with compassion, oh honey, I love you, too.

Obedient daughters eat their dinners alone—and harshly isolated.

Kaufman's amputation pornography, she was exactly like her Stein.

Her sleeping sea urchin could only lose ten pounds.

Milton's *Paradise Lost* in the realm of spinal amalgamation.

The musculature of a daydreaming animal lost in thoughts.

Retallack's magic rule of nine and the decimal system.

Umlaut behavior and the massive éclat of somnambulant cowboys.

The bio mimicry of elliptical ice terriers' parallel curves.

Terrifying and reciprocal alterity actually happening in real time.

All life has been a preparation for this moment.

I look at the canvas and I start painting.

Now I am a solitary loner, barely denying it.

If silence is a form of speech, then speech . . .

Demand openness and open doors with another open door.

Blessings will come again soon, let's graciously not complain.

Every moment matters, we were lovely, the lights on.

California Dexedrine Las Palmas I will not be sick.

Stop-the-car-near-the-ocean-goodbye-forever poem.

An essay concerning human understanding John Locke volume two.

The supposition that words have a certain evident signification.

Ideas, also of substances, must be made of things.

A gentle and kind orangutan represents my personal death.

Avoiding constriction of internal formations by limiting one's
options.

How two different beliefs occur in two different heads.

We eventually calm down without understanding the mechanism
involved.

Yentsia bakoondy eeleck, ta-dee-doo-dah, bentsey la cozy fen-fen.

Bit baloon timi zin zah, timi zin zah, zimbudah.

I'm a conduit between my surroundings and my output.

We all operate simultaneously and together on different levels.

Thoughts clear enough to land on paper do so.

Understand me as a continuity rather than a changelessness.

I'm going to the store, do you need anything?

A slumbering kangaroo who is capable of wordless thinking.

Nothing compares to the bubbling of a blubby blabber.

One thing is certain: use it *and* lose it.

Invent a Self who will then invent other Selves.

18

Certain forms are available to us only in discourse.

The thing is that we all just fall apart.

Overexposed concretized language, primary writing, a caress was enough.

Happiness is just one of those words people use.

Intense project feminist critique progressively pissed them off mightily.

Was it a business move reinforcing hierarchies, Ron's blog.

Esteem recognition salute honor rave regard appreciation notice value.

Imagine the intersection where language and reality might meet.

Fluctuating life caught in the "endless flow of becoming."

66

One two three four La Cumparsita the old tango.

Calm serious civilized people stare thoughtfully at the floor.

Humiliation, and the shame it brings, fills my heart.

The difference between negotiating the stairs and not is critical.

The sloshing of warm water resembles and reassembles us.

Stacy Ess Zee's comfort versus deadly fatal bodily discomfort.

The Moondance Diner and the Weird-but-True Section.

A reflection of the Self now reflecting on itself.

The now—always the now—always the same now.

Love is found in all the ways friends speak.

Vacillating between what is possible and what actually happens.

Bouncing between understandable resistance and the inevitable
eventual progression.

What makes you think that living is not dying?

An overexcited person cannot see or hear very clearly.

Glacial scorn inside our throats worsened by our contentions.

California dreaming and a dreamy dream for future
rememberings.

The future sits loosely enclosed inside the human mind.

Because it's good to leave some time between pieces.

The act of writing has reversed the empty space.

And death can always come in the next minute.

The notion of form and formlessness is being contemplated.

Music is heard through headphones near a brick wall.

Discourse aligns itself along multiple staves of the score.

Everyone knows that common sense is direct and primitive.

All sorts of origins are being ascribed to structures.

The infinitely increasing distance between everything and
   everything else.

And then suddenly Pouf, it's all gone, you see.

You see how interchangeable and reversible how pliable delicate.

The keyboard's keys are the tentacles of the matrix.

The fractal pattern of which we are a part.

The human body as a cumbersome and genial vehicle.

Nobody enjoys being tossed overboard suddenly and without
warning.

Flaubert to Sand: *l'homme c'est rien, l'oeuvre c'est tout.*

The human being is nothing, the work is everything.

Another way of saying *ars longa, vita brevis est.*

And here is the ninth line, not saying much.

Be careful out there, bundle up: trust your instinct.

Demystification through writing and a constant calling into question.

Making what is unspoken speak by touching without grasping.

Steely and forbidding situations are often met with reserve.

What an extraordinary privilege it is to be here!

Porn sites searchable by fetish, the need for intimacy.

The impulse to revolt lurking just under the surface.

I turn inward, loss of uncertainty, the incest taboo.

I sense the mysterious unknowable present at my fingertips.

Hear the lovely baby grand piano at my feet.

Feel the sounds, hear the music, sense the moment.

Feel those feelings and mostly keep them to yourself.

Sense the obsession and take a distance from it.

I read as I possibly can, to tell myself.

I tell myself to possibly read, as I can.

Believe it when I tell you an inner truth.

Listen to these words and the sounds they make.

Imagine having an appetite and not finding any food.

I avail myself of all that's available to me.

To be elaborately bypassed and left out really stings.

Trying to help one friend shouldn't necessitate hurting another.

Well what did I expect, what did I expect?

The pleasure of power and the intoxication of lying.

A chance to look at me before I walk.

Impending ending at safe distance, a chance to sleep.

The subtext of certain reticent writing must remain inaccessible.

Viable children must kill their parents to make room.

Often when I say "you" I really mean "we."

Stylish hairdo notwithstanding, what a ridiculous character you are.

Do you feel the need to be always happy?

I'm afraid stupid Cupid bit me in the ass.

Now I am completely powerless to redirect my attention.

The sphere of the private, the erotic, the repressed.

The false Self, the as-if personality, the trivial matter.

Jackson was blessed with perfect kindness in his heart.

Our cat understood this reality as a direct experience.

This could be the happiest day of my life.

You never know when such a thing might happen.

You have to be open to such a thing.

And death can always come in the next minute.

I know I said this before—it bears repeating.

Distant elements resurrect old patterns within our current organisms.

Fear, love, hatred, and the passive emotion of indolence.

Remember, with me, you can forget about the context.

Revision honors the fact that ideas exist in time.

Wiki Mandolin stole his happiness from an indifferent universe.

Determinism is not the enemy but the relentless ego.

Folie a deux figurine, funny little dinky ink blob.

I'm only good when I'm good for nothing.

The gym makes me feel like I'm a member.

You say that the perfect act has no results.

If I can understand it, anyone can understand it.

Those FedEx guys lost their cool completely that day.

Ziglio lusty mannequin gooey saliva shiva tzim-tzim tchebaba.

Tchebaba society self knowledge through doglike valor celery
  belittled.

I could create a whole circus inside your head.

Plus drive you, like a New York cabbie would.

Out of love he wants to die—*aus Liebe*.

Day in terror and then frequent flyer miles everywhere.

The promise of a beach and the fulfillment thereof.

Eggy ambition cleverly framed inside a pale ginger device.

Zip me up and examine my brain cells carefully.

He kept an illegitimate mistress, a silly little secret.

As far as the eye can see, you speak.

Precious dusk precious glimmer foxy dusk perfectly perilous dusk.

Hungry fox threw a fleeting glimpse at the exit.

I've nothing better to do than be here now.

Handsful of degenerative sandy cantankerous infantilizations, past and future.

To be recognized by a snake is an honor.

Boredom dismay agony confusion, let the poem take over.

Thick fleshy melancholy tenebrating gingerbread, but who is talking?

Diagnostic difficulties, jellybean etiquette, ziplock flew between those legs.

The apartment is the form into which I fit.

I keep within the boundaries of the apartment like nothing.

I must leave the apartment and I must return.

Dualistic self-contradictory conflictedness disjunctively forming a
  sense of counterenlightenment.

What if I've said everything I'll ever have said?

Internal excitement buzz pleasure thrill zest gratification luxury bliss.

Ruthless egoism of the will, so you can breathe.

Ancient pulmonary carbonite magnification, as if we didn't know.

One of us is bound to be the one.

I will write these until something else comes along.

"These," being the Nines, of which this is 32.

Leslie Scalapino died last night—we listen to her.

Focus attention on something without focusing on the outcome.

Why I feel like an intruder in your life.

Scatter your things, and soon you'll scatter your thoughts.

The truth! you misanthrope, the truth! only the truth!

Vacillating between accepting the newborn or giving it away.

Elaborate and complex seduction ritual on a daily basis.

Touch me, stalk me, smell me out, suggest me.

Feel fondle hold hug kiss lick and "everything" me.

Shanghai me, print me, blow my mind, flabbergast me.

Drop my name, ooze, chime, percolate my varnish remover.

Pave my way, determine me, come live with me.

I am paved with pebbles, callously acute crunchy pebbles.

Rigid uncompromising harsh obdurate intransigent rigorous
  endlessly hard pebbles.

Impeccable outcome trespass ill-timed and definitely malfeasant
  duality.

Multitasking polylingual bone-crunching tenacious backbreaking
  traces of pebbles.

And then the connection between them was suddenly severed.

Energy equals guts equals quicksand-always-possible, equals contingency.

Alphabets cross tradition from human mind to human mind.

Nine is the largest single digit, should anyone wonder.

Speech sounds of language, symbols and modifiers, articulatory considerations.

Funky feline insomnia petulant bonbon Zigamoff polymorphic celebration reference.

All of us crazed, wild, panicky, as supplies dwindle.

The morass, the desert, the wasteland, the uranium mine.

Flashing teeth among tirelessly negotiated deals—yes, I'm hurting.

I'm inside the very hole I dug for myself.

Indifferent universalism inhibits delinquent distance-runners and
their fans.

Even liars will shoot the truth sometimes, by necessity.

Shobogenzo needless worry—total activity of life and death.

Short intense bursts of compassionate anguish followed by
espousal.

Thingamajig of the memory bank from which I draw.

As the Nines turn into a narration, I narrate.

Thirteen doodads double-dared and defenestrated by accumulating
singularities.

"No matter, we shall have loved each other well."

I might be able to tell my life story.

You never know when such a thing might happen.

The complex history that defined Annie Brigitte Gilles Tardos.

French kid with a Hungarian father and Austrian mother.

She was five when they left France for Hungary.

She was twelve when she moved to Vienna, alone.

Luckily, her mother's two Viennese sisters were living there.

Muddy-faced boozer and a thin film of dust.

"She eased the ball-shaped doodad back into its socket."

Drawn back to France at 18, I move there.

Difficult times, spectacular migraine headaches, pennylessness,
    solitude and despair.

This isn't easy to talk about, even for me.

Trying to embrace the narrative turn this poem takes.

It's not like someone else suggested it to me.

"Write your autobiography, why don't you, it's so fascinating."

Each time I tackled this before, I soon bailed.

Might be able to face it as a "Nine."

Flight be stable, you fake it as a spine.

Born in Cannes, smack into the French Resistance movement.

Red-diaper babies tend to quickly learn what's what.

My situation must have been everything but pleasantly relaxing.

It's hard enough to have to be a child . . .

My function was to please my mother, by existing.

After a while these things tend to wear off.

My roles were manifold and still not completely determined.

It's touch-something-rotten-and-get-your-hands-dirty.

Or else I'm-paralyzed-with-sadness-fear-and-sorrow.

I survived everything so why do I feel defeated?

The rule of the game is that we lose.

Because the meaning of life is that it stops.

And the meaning of stopping is that we're living.

The eccentric biography will have to be sprinkled in.

Russian school in Hungary, French school in Austria—true.

The artist controls what she allows into her work.

Teeth clenched, she pushes and pulls until something breaks.

A danger to herself, the artist decides to stop.

Take a good look, she says about her inventory.

Palatially housed, her inflammatory and multifaceted set of selves.

Old brain inside the new brain, inside the skull.

The exact velocity of quantum particles cannot be known.

Like wave equations in the space of certain dimensions.

I never thought that things would go this far.

Angular momentum of closely-knit and sexually adventurous people.

Any piece of matter, when heated, starts to glow.

It's that kind of relationship that's built on friction.

I return to Vienna and I study film-making.

But also, I'm a puppeteer at the Vienna Puppet Theater.

Old grotesque decadent Germanic reality imposed upon Javanese
puppets.

The French were less complicated, the Americans even less.

Nietzsche was easy to find, easy to read there.

Then came New York and the *Art Students League*.

Years of sculpture, mural painting, anatomy, and Renaissance
perspective.

After the *League*, I decide to make video art.

Ever wonder if they'll torture you at the end?

Masochism has been my biggest and most subtle enemy.

Every word is the last one I'll ever utter.

I'm realistic, I forget the Self, I perceive justly.

My confused, conscious being is both here and elsewhere.

I am defined entirely by the languages I speak.

And the languages, in turn, are defined by me.

Speaking the fibrillative body-language is a regular nail-biter.

Silence emerges diaphonically from my every orifice, this moment.

This is definitely very hard work, all this here.

Men are big and cumbersome and always there, inevitably.

Not clear why I stay with writing 9-word lines.

Seems to work for me on an intangible level.

Since we're unattached to notions of "like" or "dislike."

As if we were holding hands in the dark.

Plenty of continuity is needed to create an object.

At lower levels, higher realities appear as images, shadows.

One finite instant of possible lifeforms, eternally hovering options.

Michelin figure ridicule, and who is ashamed of whom.

Too often my view of suffering is sexually charged.

Sabine Domec was born in the Champagne. Sephardic Jews.

Suffering, mercifully, offers a route back into the ego.

The ego then actively abandons suffering and we're free.

Dear Lyn, yes, Buddhism, I see the need, indeed.

Norman, aka Normal, was both gentle and firm, then.

Watch the lips and fingers do whatever they want.

Community-theft ambience, slithering-rigmarole-pizzazz, bellicose
Ramos Fizz.

If you think ill of others, that's *your* idea.

The point of any action—the invention—No point.

Random walks we could take in seemingly random forests.

Direction lozenge apprehension tension, whatever you will with me.

With me it's every chance I get to act.

Act as if you're dead already, they tell me.

Say it with infinite sincerity indigo serpent reflected sun.

Sun-dried kisses, valedictorian elements, unintended profanities
  hurled at me.

I love it when you pry into my life.

The ninth line is often problematic, as we see.

After a while you learn to tone it down.

Fear resembling moss, moss resembling tree, tree resembling
vegetable.

Random elements of chance cannot be analyzed any further.

Made off with everyone's money and went to prison.

Things will never be resolved until galaxies stop colliding.

What makes you think I'm not wearing a tuxedo?

Pseudo fanatic simplification applied to chemical processes
basic form.

Each metaphorically motivated concept forms and influences
each move.

Reasonable Avalokiteshvara fidgety lifetime contribution using
the mind.

47

My relational individuality is defined by all the specifics.

It's hard to get things right, to believe them.

Mental distortions symbolize steadily evolving habits, make me cry.

Anticipating total collapse of barriers, user-friendly people
    have babies.

I'm wondering about the next step: what is it?

An immense yearning for escape and all its consequences.

I see myself as a tourist, doing the sites.

So where is this autobiography, I'm beginning to wonder.

I would sit down at the piano and think.

Daring investors sink fortunes into their thought patterns.

So how do you like your future, Ms. Tardos?

Not bad at all, I like it a lot.

The requirements of life take me farther and farther.

Again and again, and again and again, and again.

I feel understood and not understood all at once.

In any case, the universe works exactly this way.

Memory and contemplation, the infinite language of my life.

I want to, but can't get outside of myself.

49 (for Steve Benson)

In this other room, I begin to count words.

I change involuntarily and incessantly, counting up to nine.

I lean into one kind of attention or another.

My strange companion lives inside my frame of mind.

Something that doesn't exist exists, just think about it.

Symbolizing existence's continuous existence, its own self,
as example.

This poisonous effluvia, this baffling despair in our souls.

Confused, illiterate thoughts infiltrate the mind, call themselves
"demons."

The horror of being alone in bed at night.

50 (for S. B.)

By inserting my text into yours, I lengthen both.

Thoughts matter to thoughts, as cats matter to birds.

Unable to sleep, I frighten myself with outlandish scenarios.

Ounce of strength—frame of mind—soul of truth.

Underbelly of intimacy, the zealous indiscretion of the living.

I concomit your text with mine, splitting it apart.

I am you, and you are me, whatever happens.

Hurricanes torment palms, toss rocks around, kill birds.

I'm afraid of becoming too intimate with this thing.

51 (for K.G.)

So Kenny Goldsmith picks up a book, any book.

And yes, I'm guilty of the same problem.

An exquisitely personal writing machine for one's own genius.

With minutes to go, he will have killed genius.

Brion Gysin couldn't escape this nutritionlessness and
    valuelessness.

Mac Low made personal choices, it's just the opposite.

Poetry for inhuman readers who do not yet exist.

I am an original genius with tragically bad timing.

Genius genius genius genius genius genius genius genius genius.

52 (for C.B.)

Charles Bernstein, the final speaker at this phenomenological
   intersection.

Yet whenever he does that, he gets that silence.

Those excruciatingly long fifteen seconds, I mean, as if…

He chose Larry Eigner, finally an incompetent, after all.

There was just one earlier book, very small, 1953.

The typewriter he got for a Bar Mitzvah present.

Being the least cosmopolitan of people in the 1950s.

He writes a dead-dog poem: "The Dead Dog."

Finally meeting Creeley, the end of a beautiful poem.

53 (for R.B.D.)

Rachel Blau DuPlessis spent 5 francs and 25 centimes.

Her door opened to a masculinist referentiality transforming reality.

Second Avenue's visceral erotic pulse simply charming
  Frank O'Hara.

The name of a street for a traveling poem.

Comedy and insouciance in contrast to the heroine's aboutness.

Pink and speedy Larry Rivers, happening all at once.

Had a real nice party going on next door.

A message to the Self, a totally other zone.

John Ashbery's most important deck-clearing move was made.

54 (for C.F.)

Crotchety old Chris Funkhouser concentrates on manifest
  hedonistic sexuality.

Buddhism urges me to find compassion for this man.

I was indeed *not* referencing Keats, and said so.

Jackson Mac Low's rainy life, the outside, the void.

His identity normally associated with this or that movement.

Connective tissues to the Beats found weirdly and amusingly.

Seeing Mac Low's efforts as a rejection of materialism.

A copy of the book in your precious hands.

A reading, commemorating an observation, an homage,
  a silence.

55 (for E.K.)

Erica Kaufman welcomes Guest to her Location of Things.

Architecture, the defining element in an otherwise diffuse space.

Illusions of stability, Barbara's female text, genderedness of
humanity.

Language without transcendence participates in a domestically
divergent reality.

Am I to understand change, whether remarkable or hidden.

The binary realities of our male contemporaries' dominant
masculinity.

Anachronistic reminders by Yi-Fu Tuan: "page as pictorial space."

Love, romance, and a man's protection cannot possibly suffice.

Writing as an act of differentiation and of participation.

56 (for R.S.)

The Duncan Ron first met in 1966 argued adamantly.

Poems Opening the Field, the lover Jess, re opening.

I have no good prospects for finding a publisher.

I propose a writing as continuous as the Cantos.

To set the stage for the best possible reception.

Duncan found the need to break down parts within.

"Often" he was "permitted to return to a meadow."

At the *Museum of Modern Art* in the 1980s.

Enraged by video cameras at his reading he explodes.

Baby-Billy bathwater bubbles to the surface below California.

Santergiggly, what did you say, interfering money-hungry kangaroos.

Idée fixe indefinitely feministic writing entertaining notions
of intertextuality.

Different kinds of writing, *fouliaskabar* gentrifying syntax-free
obligations.

Super siren, lonely bourbon, polylingual guessing work despite itself.

Tailwind monkey-zipper leaning forward, ingesting whatever
comes along.

Out of the blue and out of thin air.

Zin-zen generation, pugnacious birthright obligation, realistically
speculative thinking.

Destructo flirtation or else let me take a shower.

Frozen handcuffs bound intoxicatingly bitter winter hinterland
all alone.

A full philosophical account of human life and language.

It may turn out that we need each other.

Mine is a mind that stays balanced and even.

First things first, take it easy, easy does it.

And after all, who do I think I am.

I want to live with *you*, not your addiction.

The immense attraction to the material envelope of satisfaction.

Genderbending trivia simplification, and that was only three words.

Aghast at the flesh-eating-flesh state of affairs.

Stuffing those savage stomachs with nourishment wrought
from destruction.

I must view myself as a god or perish.

We may never know the origin of the universe.

Now that I found happiness again, I recognize you.

During all of my unusual life, I knew you.

New events turn out to be ancient ones, repeating.

Ancient Europe dusty dewrope newrope insecurope pureope
sureope endureope.

And why am I writing everything in nines, anyway.

The steady gaze of the elephant in the room.

Topsy turvy trust issues undermine questions of self love.

The perfect listener is both delightfully attentive and deferential.

Too much reticence can freeze your heart and mine.

You're my hippocampus, the sea-horse I can't live without.

It's either going to be tartar sauce or puttanesca.

Effervescent joviality can fade like decayed euphoria almost
  instantly.

Instant remembrances approach me like trees in the forest.

Inadmissible lines containing more or fewer words than nine.

It might be appropriate to mention my father again.

Communist Hungarian writer imprisoned by communist Hungarian regime, 1957.

He and other writers in solitary over two years.

I'm twelve and being sent to Vienna for safety.

Louis Aragon pleads for the writers' release in Moscow.

Moscow listens and my father moves to Paris, 1960.

I barely comprehend this but now I get it.

Confusion dismay horror disbelief incomprehension alarm distress adolescent girlhood.

Anxiety funk depression helplessness defiance pugnacious insubordination and humiliation.

They broke his spirit and he wrote about it.

My mother was more of a mystery to me.

European Jews miraculously surviving the Nazi persecution became communists.

Not all, but many had nowhere else to turn.

Until the tide turned and the disillusionment came about.

The awakening that turned so many against the Party.

And turned their beliefs upside down and inside out.

Overnight, they went from one extreme to the other.

Shame embarrassment humiliation contradictions more uncertainties for the Jews.

I wasn't even told we were Jewish, until later.

Because Europeans couldn't take any chances in those days.

I was born in Cannes, in hiding, in fear.

After the war, my mother became a radio producer.

I listened to her live broadcasts, alone, after school.

Alone, I listened to my mother on the radio.

You might say I was being neglected a bit.

I became someone who had to grow up fast.

Only later to shrink herself, like Alice, to fit.

ROOF BOOKS

the best in language since 1976

Selected & Recent Titles

- Fodaski, Elizabeth. **Document**. 80p. $13.95
- Gordon, Nada. **Scented Rushes**. 104p. $13.95
- Kuszai, Joel. **Accidency**. 120 p. $14.95.
- Retallack, Joan. **Procedural Elegies/Western Civ Cont/**. 120p. $14.95.
- Torres, Edwin. **Yes Thing No Thing**. 128 p. $14.95.
- Vallejo, César. Translated by Joseph Mulligan.
  Against Professional Secrets. 104 p. $14.95.

ROOF BOOKS are published by
Segue Foundation
300 Bowery • New York, NY 10012
Visit our website at **seguefoundation.com**

ROOF BOOKS are distributed by
SMALL PRESS DISTRIBUTION
1341 Seventh Street • Berkeley, CA. 94710-1403.
Phone orders: 800-869-7553
spdbooks.org